WAYS INTO HISTORY

Houses and Homes

Sally Hewitt

W

FRANKLIN WATTS
LONDON • SYDNEY

This edition 2006
First published in 2004 by
Franklin Watts
338 Euston Road
London NW1 3BH

Franklin Watts Australia
Hachette Children's Books
Level 17/207 Kent Street
Sydney, NSW 2000

© Franklin Watts 2004

ISBN-13: 978 0 7496 5579 2

Series Editor: Sally Luck
Art Director: Jonathan Hair
Design: Rachel Hamdi/Holly Mann
Picture Research: Diana Morris

A CIP catalogue record for this book is available
from the British Library.

Picture credits
Photography by Chris Fairclough unless otherwise credited.
AP/Topham: 25tr.
Andrew J G Bell/Eye Ubiquitous: front cover r, 7cr, 9r.
Michael Boys/Corbis: 7tr, 14, 15tl.
Canadian Museum of Civilization/Corbis: 17cr.
Clark/Topham: 13.
Ashley Cooper/Picimpact/Corbis: 26tr.
Hulton Archive: 18.
Kurt Hutton/Hulton Archive: 21t.
Lambert/Hulton Archive: front cover bl, 24.
Philippa Lewis/Edifice/Corbis: 7cl, 15tr, 15cr.
Clay Perry/Corbis: 10t.
Picturepoint/Topham: 3, 7tl, 8t, 10c,11, 16, 22, 23cr, 25cl, 25cr, 27.
Private Collection/Bridgeman Art Library: 21c.
Science Museum, London/HIPS   Topham: 17tr, 19cl, 23cl.
Adam Woolfitt/Corbis: 19tl.

Every attempt has been made to clear copyright. Should there
be any inadvertent omission, please apply to
the publisher for rectification.

Printed in China

Franklin Watts is a division of Hachette Children's Books.

Contents

A home is where you live with your family. It is where you keep your things.

Your home protects you from the weather. You feel safe there.

💬 Talk about...

...what you do at home.
Use these words to help you:

play	eat	sleep
wash	talk	read

Homes can look very different.
But most homes have some
things that are the same.

A window

A front door

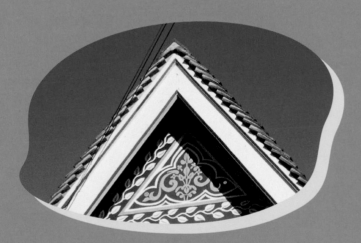

A roof

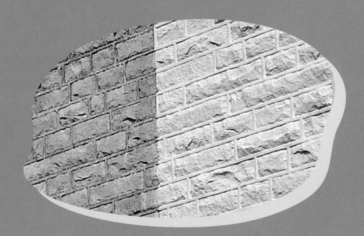

Walls

A front door lets you in and out. What
do roofs, walls and windows do?

Look at the homes around your area.
What else can you see on the outside?
Is your home old or new?

All kinds of homes

There are all kinds of homes. Bungalows only have one floor. A tall block of flats can have 20 floors, or more!

A bungalow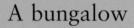

◁ A block of flats

Why do you think flats are often built in crowded cities?

How many homes do you think are in this block of flats?

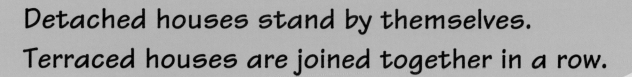

Detached houses stand by themselves.
Terraced houses are joined together in a row.

△ Detached house

Terraced
houses ▷

🔍 Be a historian...

Look at the pictures of homes on these pages.

Do you think they were built at the same time?

What is the same about them?

What is different?

What kind of home do you live in?

Great and small

Longleat House was built more than 400 years ago.

Longleat ▷
House

Inside, there is a great hall, a dining room, seven libraries and lots of other rooms!

◁ The drawing room

🔍 Be a historian…

How many rooms do you think there are inside Longleat House?

What kind of people do you think lived here?

This little cottage was built at the same time as Longleat House. It has two rooms downstairs and two rooms upstairs.

Who do you think lived in this cottage?

💬 **Talk about...**

...what it would be like to live in these different homes.
Which would you rather live in?
Can you say why?

Inside, homes are usually divided into rooms.
We do different things in different rooms.

What rooms can you see in this plan of a flat?
What rooms do you have in your home?
What do you do in these rooms?

Some houses have one big room where you relax, cook and eat. It is a kitchen, a living room and a dining room – all in one!

Why do you think a room like this is called "open-plan"?

Q Talk about...

… your favourite room in your house.

Use these words to help you:

cosy	colourful	noisy
quiet	comfortable	play

Built to last

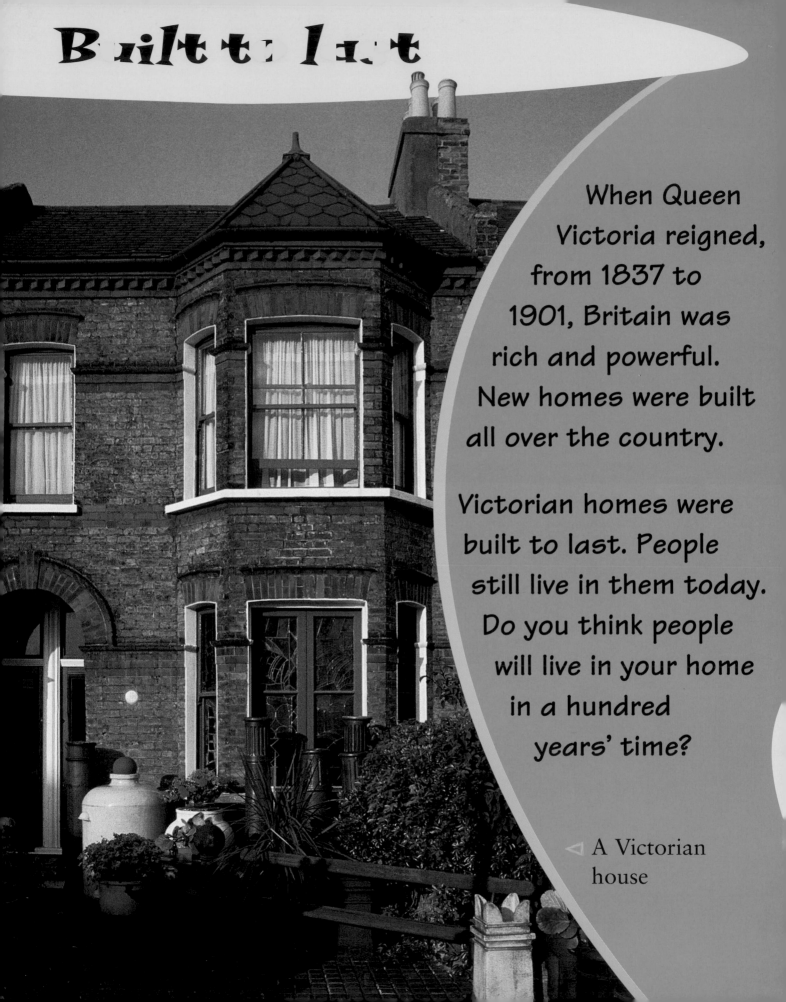

When Queen Victoria reigned, from 1837 to 1901, Britain was rich and powerful. New homes were built all over the country.

Victorian homes were built to last. People still live in them today. Do you think people will live in your home in a hundred years' time?

◁ A Victorian house

The Victorians built their houses with brick, plaster, tiles, wood and glass.

Wooden window frames

A brick chimney

Tiles

🔍 Be a historian...

Look back at the other houses in this book. What materials do you think they were built with?

Many Victorian houses had patterns and decorations on the outside. What do you think they looked like inside? Turn the page to find out...

The living room

Rooms in Victorian homes were full of furniture and ornaments. Everything was covered in patterns and decorations.

△ A Victorian living room

The lady in the picture is reading. What else do you think a Victorian family did in their living room? What do you do in your living room?

You can tell which room you are in by looking at the things in it. These four things belong in a living room.

Be a historian...

Which objects in the pictures could belong in...
- your living room?
- a Victorian living room?
- either living room?

In the kitchen

Kitchen maids had to work hard in
Victorian times. Look at the picture.
What jobs are the maids doing?
What other jobs do you think they did?

▽ Victorian maids
working in the
kitchen of a
wealthy
home

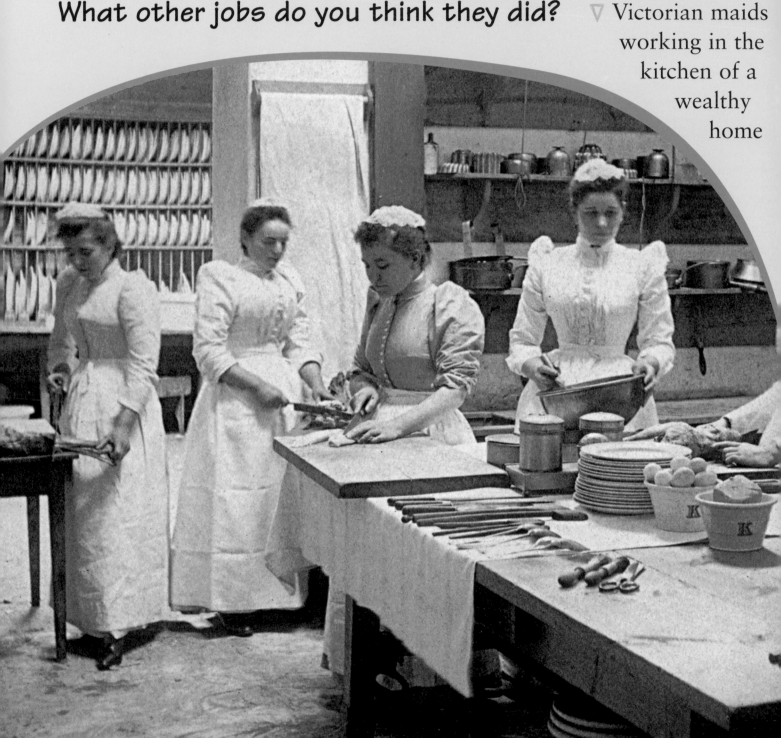

Today we use electric machines, like irons
and kettles. There was no electricity
in a Victorian kitchen.

Electric
kettle

Victorian kettle

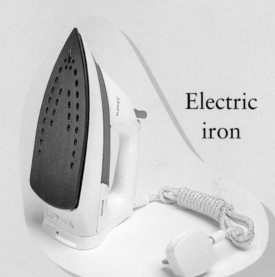

Electric
iron

Victorian bellows and a box iron

Be a historian...

Victorians placed burning charcoal inside
a box iron to heat it. They used bellows to fan
air into the iron to keep the charcoal glowing.
Do you think a box iron would be easy to use?
Can you say why?
Why do electric machines make things easy?

Bedroom

Your bedroom is where you sleep.
You probably keep your clothes
and toys there.

Does your bedroom look like this?
What is in your bedroom?
Do you share your bedroom?

In some Victorian houses, the children in the family all shared the same bed. Do you think it was fun being a child in Victorian times?

A chamber pot was kept under the bed. Can you guess what it was for?

🔍 Be a historian...
Most Victorian houses did not have tap water. How do you think Victorians washed and went to the toilet? Turn the page to find out...

Washing and cleaning

Water often had to be fetched from a pump in the street. Toilets were in the garden. Women washed clothes by hand outside.

▽ Washing clothes with a mangle, around 1900

Talk about...

... how the women in the picture are washing clothes. Use these words to help you:

mangle   soap   squeeze   rinse   water

Victorians invented new cleaning tools and machines, like the mangle. In the 20th century, there were even more inventions.

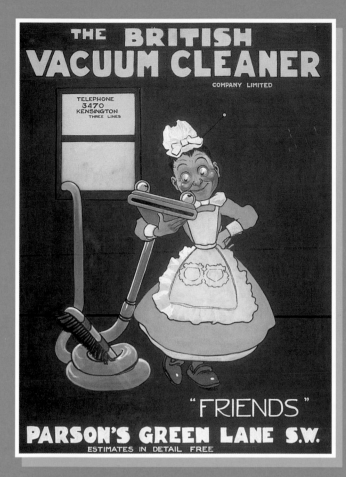

△ Advertisement for a vacuum cleaner, 1908

△ Advertisement for a new style of mop, 1918

🔍 Be a historian...

How do you think people cleaned floors before mops and vacuum cleaners were invented? What other machines do we use for cleaning?

New homes

During the 1950s many new homes were built.
They had modern kitchens and bathrooms.
Some even had garages for cars.

For the first time, many families could
afford a new piece of furniture for the
living room – a television!

By the 1950s, lots of homes had telephones and radios. A few had washing machines.

🔍 Be a historian...

How do you think life in a 1950s' home was different from life in a Victorian home?

Find some people who can remember the 1950s.

Ask them what their homes were like.

Old and new

Today, many old houses are still lived in, but some are pulled down to make room for brand new houses.

Some new homes are built to look like old ones. Do the houses in this picture remind you of any others in this book?

This is a very modern house. It has solar panels that use energy from the Sun to heat water. Many houses might look like this in the future.

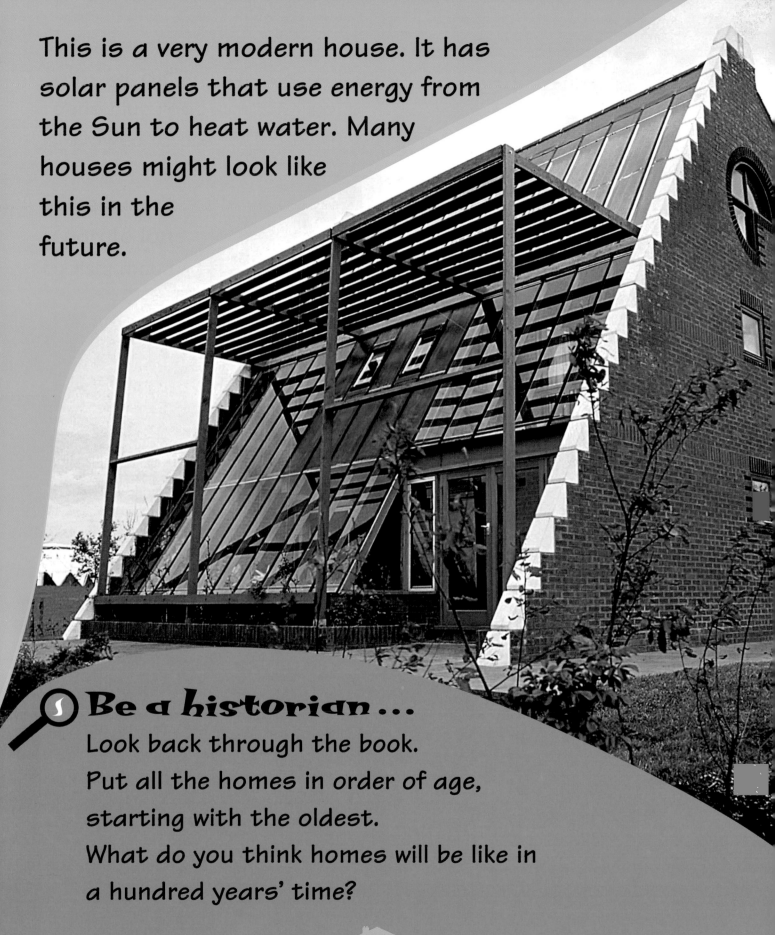

🔍 Be a historian...

Look back through the book.
Put all the homes in order of age, starting with the oldest.
What do you think homes will be like in a hundred years' time?

Timeline

Start

1500s–1800s
Stately homes, cottages and town houses are built.

1837 – 1901
Queen Victoria rules Britain. Many new homes are built all over the country.

The late 1800s
Household machines, like mangles, are invented.

1907
The first electric vacuum cleaner is invented.

1950s
Lots of homes have their first television, radio, and washing machine.

Today
Modern homes are being designed and built. Some have solar panels.

1960s
Tall blocks of flats are built in towns and cities.

End

Glossary

Electricity
A kind of power that comes into our homes through wires, or is stored in batteries.

Invention
A new idea for a design that no one has thought of before.

Machine
Something that makes work easier. A cooker and an iron are both types of machine.

Materials
What things are made of. Glass, brick and plaster are building materials.

Modern
Things that are modern have been built or made very recently.

Ornaments
Vases and china figures are kinds of ornaments used to decorate a room.

Plaster
A powder mixed with water that is put over walls to make them smooth.

Pump
A pipe with a lever that is moved up and down to bring water up from under ground.

Index